kids'
meals & snacks

NEW
HOLLAND

contents

introduction

This is a cookbook with a difference: the recipes were chosen by children for children. Children helped to test them and it was the majority view that decided what should be included.

The result is a well-balanced selection of recipes for all ages and all occasions. Brains with parsley sauce and tripe and onions got the thumbs down, but the panel approved plenty of salads, wholefood bakes, fruity desserts and vegetarian dishes alongside old favourites such as kebabs, pizza, pasta and chicken drumsticks as well as sweet treats such as rocky road ice cream and lamingtons.

Breakfasts and lunches came in for careful scrutiny, with the accent on speedily prepared dishes for school days and some special treats for weekends. Dinners are more substantial, but also take into account the pit-stop factor—some dishes can be made in minutes while others can safely be put on hold for late-comers.

Healthy school lunches are an important part of helping your kids make the most of their school day—they need good food to help them grow, learn and play. Their day should, however, be a mix of learning and fun, so what they find in their lunchboxes should not only be healthy but also something they look forward to.

Keeping it fresh, simple and healthy is the key to a fun lunchtime for all.

snacks

Cheese triangles

MAKES 4

10 oz (300 g) ricotta cheese
10 oz (300 g) feta cheese
4 eggs
white pepper
1 packet filo pastry
4 oz (115 g) melted butter

1. Pre-heat the oven to 400°F/200°C/Gas mark 6.
2. Combine the ricotta, feta and eggs in a bowl and mix well. Season with pepper.
3. Brush one layer of filo pastry with melted butter, and place another layer on top.
4. Cut the pastry, lengthwise, into 4 strips. To shape the triangles, place a heaped teaspoon of cheese mixture close to the bottom of the right-hand corner of the strip. Fold this corner, diagonally across to the left-hand edge over the mixture to form a triangle. Continue folding from right to left in a triangular shape to the end of strip.
5. Brush the top of the triangle with the melted butter and place on a baking tray (sheet). Repeat until all the mixture has been used up.
6. Bake for about 20 minutes or until golden.

Chicken with sesame seeds

SERVES 4

1 tablespoon sesame oil
1 teaspoon five spice powder
1 lb (450 g) chicken tenderloins, halved
2 tablespoon cornflour (cornstarch), for
 dusting
peanut oil
3 tablespoons honey
1 tablespoon lemon juice
2 tablespoons sesame seeds

BATTER
1 oz (30 g) cornflour (cornstarch)
3 oz (85 g) self-raising (self-rising) flour
½ pint (300 ml) water
1 egg white

1. Mix the sesame oil with the five spice powder and brush over the chicken. Leave for 15 minutes.
2. To make the batter, sift the flours into a bowl. Add the water and mix until smooth.
3. In a separate bowl, beat the egg white until stiff, and fold into the batter.
4. Pour a small amount of peanut oil into a wok or large frying pan and place over medium heat.
5. Dip a piece of chicken into the cornflour, shake off the excess, dip into the batter and place immediately into the hot oil. Repeat with 5 or 6 more pieces. Cook until golden brown, then place on a plate lined with absorbent paper. Repeat with remainder.
6. Drain all the oil from the wok. Add the honey and lemon juice to the wok and warm through on medium heat. Add the chicken piece a few at a time and coat with the honey mixture. Remove to a serving platter and scatter the sesame seeds on top. Serve hot.

Chicken nuggets

MAKES 24

1 lb (450 g) minced (ground) chicken
1 egg, lightly beaten
1½ oz (45 g) fresh breadcrumbs
2 oz (55 g) cottage cheese, mashed
4 oz (115 g) dried breadcrumbs
vegetable oil, for shallow frying

1. Put the chicken, egg, fresh breadcrumbs and cottage cheese in a bowl and mix well to combine. Take 2 tablespoons of mixture, shape into a ball, then flatten slightly.
2. Pour the dried breadcrumbs onto a large plate. Gently press each nugget into the dried breadcrumbs to coat all sides. Repeat until all the chicken mixture is used up.
3. Heat ½ in (1 cm) of oil in a frying pan over a medium heat until hot, add the nuggets and cook for 2 minutes on each side, or until cooked through and golden. Drain on absorbent paper, cool slightly and serve.

Honey-glazed spare ribs

SERVES 8

4 lb (1.8 kg) pork spare ribs, trimmed of
  excess fat
2 tablespoons orange juice

HONEY SOY MARINADE
7 fl oz (200 ml/scant 1 cup) Chinese rice
  (white) vinegar
4 fl oz (120 ml/½ cup) soy sauce
4 fl oz (120 ml/½ cup) honey

1. To make the marinade, combine the vinegar, soy sauce and honey in a
   non-reactive (non-metal) dish. Add the ribs, toss to coat, cover and leave to
   marinate in the refrigerator for at least 4 hours.
2. Drain the ribs and reserve the marinade. Cook the ribs under a preheated
   grill (broiler) for 8–10 minutes or until the ribs are tender and golden, basting
   occasionally with reserved marinade. Place on a serving platter, cover and
   keep warm.
3. Place the remaining marinade in a saucepan, add the orange juice and bring
   to the boil. Reduce the heat and simmer for 15 minutes or until the sauce
   reduces by half. Pour sauce over the spare ribs.

Cheesy swirls

MAKES 10

14 oz (400 g) shortcrust pastry
plain (all-purpose) flour, for dusting
2 tablespoons tomato purée (paste)
½ teaspoon sugar
3½ oz (100 g) mature Cheddar cheese, grated
  (shredded)

1 oz (30 g) Parmesan, freshly grated
  (shredded)
1 egg, beaten, for glazing
vegetable oil, for greasing

1. Preheat the oven to 375°F/190°C/Gas mark 5.
2. Roll out the pastry into a square on a lightly floured surface and cut to make
   2 rectangles 8 x 10 in (20 x 25 cm).
3. Mix the tomato purée and sugar together then spread one sheet of pastry
   with the mixture. Arrange the second sheet of pastry on top, then scatter
   with the cheeses.
4. Roll up the pastry from the shorter side with the filling inside. Brush the roll
   with the egg and refrigerate for 20 minutes. Cut the roll into ten slices and
   place the swirls on greased baking sheets (trays).
5. Bake for 20 minutes or until golden. Leave on wire racks to cool slightly
   before serving.

Sausage puffs

MAKES 48

12 oz (350 g) puff pastry
vegetable oil, for greasing

CURRIED SAUSAGE FILLING
12 oz (350 g) sausage mince

1 small carrot, finely grated (shredded)
1 tablespoon fruit chutney
1 teaspoon curry powder
freshly ground black pepper
salt

1. To make the sausage filling, put all the filling in a bowl with salt and black pepper, to taste, and mix to combine. Cover and refrigerate until required.
2. Roll out the pastry to ⅛ in (3 mm) thick and cut out a 12 in (30 cm) square. Cut the pastry in half to make two rectangles.
3. Divide the filling in half then shape each into a thin sausage 12 in (30 cm) long. Place a sausage on the long edge of each pastry rectangle and roll up. Brush the edges with water to seal.
4. Cut each roll into ½ in (1 cm) slices, place on greased baking trays and bake for 12–15 minutes, or until filling is cooked and pastry is golden and puffed.

Note: These savoury puffs can be prepared to the baking stage in advance. Cover with plastic food wrap (cling film) and store in the refrigerator until required, then bake as directed.

Tuna wrap

SERVES 1

6 oz (175 g) canned tuna, drained
2 tablespoons mayonnaise
¼ avocado, diced
1 spring onion (scallion), finely sliced
1 iceberg lettuce leaf, finely shredded
1 flat bread

1. Combine the tuna, mayonnaise, avocado and spring onion together in a small bowl. Stir together.
2. Arrange the lettuce on the bread and top with the tuna mixture. Roll tightly and cut in half.

Pita pocket

SERVES 1

1 wholemeal (wholewheat) pita pocket
2 tablespoons hummus
¼ medium carrot, grated (shredded)
1 tablespoon Cheddar cheese, grated
   (shredded)
1 small cooked beetroot, grated (shredded)
¾ oz (20 g) lettuce leaves, shredded
1 tablespoon raisins or sultanas (golden
   raisins)
1 teaspoon lemon juice

1. Cut the pita pocket in half, spread each half with the hummus.
2. Mix the remaining ingredients in a bowl. Divide the mixture between each
   pocket.

Banana & date bread

SERVES 8

oil, for greasing
8 oz (225 g/2 cups) self-rising (self-raising)
   flour
1 teaspoon baking soda
pinch of salt
1 teaspoon ground cinnamon (powder)

4 oz (115 g/½ cup) superfine (caster) sugar
3½ oz (110 g/¾ cup) fresh dates, chopped
2 eggs
8 fl oz (250 ml/1 cup) milk
2 ripe bananas, mashed

1. Preheat the oven to 350°F/180°C/Gas mark 4, and grease and line the base and sides of a 9 x 5 in (23 x 13 cm) loaf tin (pan) with baking paper.
2. Sift the flour, baking soda, salt and cinnamon into a large bowl. Stir in the sugar and dates.
3. Combine the eggs, milk and bananas in a bowl and whisk until well combined. Stir the egg mixture into the dry ingredients until well combined.
4. Pour the mixture into prepared loaf tin. Bake for 40–45 minutes, or until golden and a skewer, when inserted into the centre of the cake comes out clean.
5. Leave to set in the tin for 10 minutes, then turn out onto a wire rack to go cold.

Sweet pumpkin coyotas

MAKES 8

COYOTAS DOUGH

1 lb 4 oz (565 g) plain (all-purpose) flour, plus
  extra for dusting
10 oz (300 g) butter, diced
pinch of salt

SWEET PUMPKIN FILLING

1½ lb (675 g) butternut pumpkin, peeled and
  chopped
4 oz (115 g/½ cup) brown sugar
1½ oz (45 g) butter, diced, plus extra for
  greasing

1. Preheat the oven to 400°F/200°C/Gas mark 6.
2. To make the filling, place the pumpkin in a baking dish, scatter with sugar, dot with butter and drizzle with two tablespoons of water. Cover and bake for 30–40 minutes or until the pumpkin is soft and golden. Leave to cool.
3. Meanwhile, to make the dough, place the flour, butter and salt in a food processor and process until the mixture resembles fine breadcrumbs. With the machine running, add enough cold water to form a soft dough, about 6 fl oz (175 ml/¾ cup). Turn the dough onto a lightly floured surface and knead for 10 minutes or until soft and elastic. Chill for 10 minutes.
4. Divide the dough into 16 equal pieces. Roll out each piece to form a ⅛ in (3 mm) thick round.
5. Place 1–2 tablespoons of filling in the centre of 8 of the dough rounds. Top with remaining rounds and press the edges to seal. Arrange the coyotas on greased baking trays, reduce oven temperature to 360°F/180°C/Gas mark 4 and bake for 25–30 minutes or until golden. Serve warm.

Turkey & cranberry sandwich

MAKES 1

2 teaspoons cranberry jelly
2 pieces thick-cut wholemeal (wholewheat)
   bread
25g (¾ oz) baby cos (romaine) leaves,
   shredded
2–3 slices turkey
snowpea (mangetout) sprouts

1. Spread the cranberry jelly over the bread. Place the lettuce, turkey slices and sprouts on one slice of bread. Top with the remaining slice of bread and cut in half.

Lavash wrap

MAKES 1

1 piece wholemeal (wholewheat) lavash bread
2 teaspoons wholegrain mustard
¾ oz (25 g) rocket (arugula)
1 slice ham
1 tablespoon ricotta cheese

1. Spread lavash with mustard, top with rocket and ham. Crumble over the ricotta.
2. Roll up the lavash, then cut in half.

Egg & cheese sandwich

SERVES 1

2 eggs, hard-boiled
1 slice Cheddar cheese, diced
1 sprig parsley, roughly chopped
1 tablespoon mayonnaise
2 slices thick-sliced wholegrain bread

1. In a small bowl, mash the egg, add the cheese, parsley and mayonnaise. Mix together.
2. Spread the egg and cheese mixture onto one slice of bread, top with the other slice and cut into quarters.

White bean dip

14 oz (400 g) can cannellini beans
1 clove garlic, crushed
2 fl oz (50 ml/¼ cup) extra virgin olive oil
juice of ½ lemon

1. Rinse and drain the beans. Place the beans, garlic, olive oil, and lemon juice in a food processor and process until combined. Add 1 tablespoon water and process again until smooth.
2. Serve with a selection of mini toasts, rice crackers, carrot sticks and celery sticks.

Pasta salad

SERVES 1

1½ oz (45 g/¾ cup) cooked pasta such as
    spirals or penne
1 tablespoon sweetcorn kernels
8 cherry tomatoes, halved
1 tablespoon pepitas (pumpkin seeds)
1 sprig parsley, roughly chopped
1 oz (30 g) Cheddar cheese, diced
¹/₃ oz (10 g) baby spinach
½ tablespoon olive oil
1 teaspoon lemon juice

1. Combine all the ingredients in a bowl and mix well.

Cherry tomato & baby bocconcini salad

SERVES 1

8 cherry tomatoes, halved
4 baby bocconcini (small mozzarella balls),
*   halved*
¼ Lebanese cucumber, thickly sliced
1 scallion (spring onion), sliced
1 sprig parsley, chopped
1 teaspoon olive oil

1. Combine all the ingredients in a bowl and mix thoroughly.

Waldorf salad

SERVES 4

1 green apple, cut into chunks
1 red apple, cut into chunks
1 stalk celery, sliced
5 baby cos (romaine) leaves, finely shredded
2 oz (55 g/¼ cup) mayonnaise
1 teaspoon lemon juice
1 oz (30 g/¼ cup) pecan or walnut halves

1. Combine the apples, celery and lettuce in a bowl with the mayonnaise, lemon juice and pecans or walnuts. Mix well.

Cheesy vegetable muffins

MAKES 12

2 oz (55 g) chargrilled bell pepper, in oil
8 oz (225 g/2 cups) self-rising (self-raising)
   flour
1 zucchini (courgette), grated (shredded)
1½ oz (45 g) Cheddar cheese, grated
   (shredded)
¼ bunch chives, chopped
8 fl oz (250 ml/1 cup) milk
1 egg, lightly beaten
2½ oz (70 g) butter, melted, plus extra for
   greasing

1. Preheat the oven to 400°F/200°C/Gas mark 6. Lightly grease a 12-cup muffin tray.
2. Place the pepper on absorbent paper to drain any excess oil. Slice the capsicum.
3. Sift the flour into a large bowl. Add the pepper, courgette, Cheddar and chives. Stir well to combine, then make a well in the centre. Use a fork to whisk the milk, egg and butter together in a bowl. Add to the flour mixture and use a large wooden spoon to mix until just combined—don't over-mix. Divide the mixture evenly between the muffin cups.
4. Bake for 20–25 minutes or until a skewer inserted into the centre of the muffins comes out clean. Set aside for 5 minutes before turning onto a wire rack to cool.

Salami scrolls

MAKES 12

8 oz (225 g/2 cups) self-rising (self-raising)
   flour
1 oz (30 g) butter, chilled
6 fl oz (175 ml/¾ cup) milk
¼ cup tomato paste (concentrate)
1 sprig basil, chopped
1 sprig parsley, chopped
3½ oz (100 g) salami, diced
1 medium red bell pepper (capsicum), diced
5 oz (150 g) Cheddar cheese, grated
   (shredded)

1. Preheat oven to 350°F (180°C) and line an oven tray with baking paper.
2. Place flour and butter in a bowl, use fingers to combine until it resembles breadcrumbs. Add the milk and mix together to make a soft, sticky dough. Knead lightly on a floured surface.
3. Roll dough into a 30 x 40cm (12 x 15¾in) rectangle. Spread the tomato paste over the dough, sprinkle the chopped herbs on top. Top with the salami, pepper and cheese.
4. Roll up from the long side of the dough. Using a serrated knife, cut the roll into 12 slices. Place the slices on the oven tray and bake for 25 minutes until brown.

Chicken & vegetable rolls

MAKES 20

2 sheets ready-rolled puff pastry
1 tablespoon milk
1 tablespoon sesame seeds

FILLING
1 carrot, grated (shredded)

1 courgette (zucchini), grated (shredded)
1 small onion, finely diced
9 oz (250 g) chicken mince (ground)
1 oz (30 g/½ cup) breadcrumbs
4 sprigs chives, chopped
1 egg, beaten

1. Preheat the oven to 400°F (200°C/Gas mark 6) and line a baking tray (sheet) with baking paper.
2. In a large bowl, combine the carrot, zucchini, onion, chicken, breadcrumbs, chives and egg.
3. Arrange the pastry sheets on a floured surface and cut each in half.
4. Spoon quarter of the chicken mixture lengthwise along the centre of each piece. Fold one edge of pastry over and tuck in beside the filling, then fold over the other side to make a roll, pressing down lightly to seal. Repeat with the remaining pastry and filling. Cut each roll into 3 cm (1¼ in) slices, place on the prepared baking tray, brush with milk and sprinkle with sesame seeds.
5. Bake for 25–30 minutes, or until the rolls are lightly browned and cooked through.

main meals

Speedy lasagne

SERVES 4

3 oz (85 g) packet white sauce mix
12 lasagne sheets
3 oz (85 g) mature Cheddar cheese, grated
   (shredded)

SPICY MEAT SAUCE
2 teaspoons vegetable oil, plus extra
   for greasing
1 onion, finely chopped
1 clove garlic, crushed
1 lb (450 g) lean minced (ground) beef
16 fl oz (500 ml) jar pasta sauce

1. To make the meat sauce, heat the oil in a frying pan over a medium heat, add the onion and garlic and cook for 2 minutes, or until onion is soft.
2. Add the mince and cook, stirring, for 5 minutes or until the meat is brown.
3. Add the pasta sauce, turn up the heat and bring to a simmer then simmer for 2 minutes. Set aside.
4. Make the white sauce according to the packet instructions.
5. Place four lasagne sheets in the base of a lightly greased ovenproof dish. Top with one-third of the meat sauce, then one-third of the white sauce and then four lasagne sheets. Repeat the layers, finishing with a layer of white sauce. Sprinkle with cheese and bake for 20–25 minutes, or until hot and bubbling and the top is golden.

Crunchy cutlets

SERVES 6

6 lamb cutlets, trimmed and slightly flattened
1 tablespoon vegetable oil

CRUNCHY COATING
1 egg, lightly beaten
1½ oz (45 g/¾ cup) breadcrumbs, made from
 stale bread
1 oz (30 g) cornflakes, crushed

1. Place the egg in a shallow dish. Put the breadcrumbs and crushed cornflakes in a separate dish and mix to combine.
2. Dip the cutlets in the egg, then in the breadcrumb mixture to coat.
3. Heat the oil in a frying pan over a medium heat until hot, add the cutlets and cook for 2 minutes on each side, or until cooked through and golden.

Bacon & egg pies

MAKES 12

3 sheets ready-rolled puff pastry
1 lb 2 oz (500 g) bacon, thinly sliced
12 fl oz (350 ml/1½ cups) sour cream
¼ cup parsley, chopped
12 eggs
oil, for greasing

1. Preheat the oven to 400°F (200°C/Gas mark 6) and lightly grease a 12-cup jumbo muffin tray.
2. Cut the pastry sheets into quarters. Place a square of pastry into each muffin cup.
3. Fry the bacon in a frying pan for 3–4 minutes or until lightly golden. Drain on absorbent paper and cool for 5 minutes. Divide three-quarters of the bacon evenly between the pastry shells.
4. In a bowl, whisk the sour cream and parsley until well combined, then pour over the bacon. Crack an egg on top of each pie, then top with the remaining bacon.
5. Bake for 25–30 minutes, or until the pastry is golden and the filling is cooked. Leave to set for 5 minutes before removing each pie from the muffin tray. Serve hot or cold.

Corn plants

SERVES 6

3 red bell peppers
3 yellow bell peppers
3 tablespoons balsamic vinegar
4 fl oz (120 ml/½ cup) olive oil
6 baby corn cobs
1 large onion, chopped
2 cloves garlic, chopped
7 oz (200 g) minced (ground) lamb

3 teaspoons tomato purée (paste)
3 oz (85 g) bulgur (cracked wheat)
16 fl oz (475 ml/2 cups) lamb stock
3 oz (85 g) frozen peas
3 oz (85 g) dried apricots, chopped
3 teaspoons ground coriander
salt and black pepper
watercress sprigs, to garnish

1. Preheat the oven to 400°F/200°C/Gas mark 6.
2. Slice off and discard the tops of the bell peppers and deseed. Square off the bases and stand on a baking tray (sheet) lined with baking paper.
3. Drizzle with balsamic vinegar and 1 tablespoon of the oil. Bake for 15 minutes then add the baby corn to the baking tray. Bake for 5–10 minutes, until tender.
4. Meanwhile, heat the remaining oil in a large pan, add the onion and garlic and fry for 5 minutes, or until softened. Add the minced lamb and cookon a low heat for 5 minutes, or until browned.
5. Stir in the tomato paste, bulgur, stock, peas, apricots and coriander, then season to taste. Bring to the boil, then simmer for 15 minutes or until the stock has been absorbed. Stir occasionally. Place the bell peppers on plates and fill with the lamb mixture. Insert a baby corn cob and decorate with a few watercress sprigs on the top of each one.

Egg & tuna salad

SERVES 2

4 new potatoes, halved
2 eggs, soft-boiled and quartered
6 oz (185 g) can tuna, drained
10 cherry tomatoes, halved
1¾ oz (45 g) French (green) beans
2 scallions (spring onions), chopped
1 sprig parsley, roughly chopped
1 tablespoon mayonnaise

1. Cook the potatoes until tender. Drain and leave to cool.
2. Combine the potatoes and egg in a bowl, add the remaining ingredients and gently combine. Divide between two plates.

Tropical pizza

SERVES 4

2 small pizza bases
2 fl oz (50 ml/¼ cup) tomato pasta sauce
2 slices ham
3½ oz (100 g) pineapple, diced
2 oz (55 g) Cheddar cheese, grated (shredded)
½ teaspoon oregano

1. Preheat the oven to 350°F/180°C/Gas mark 4.
2. Spread the pizza bases with the tomato sauce. Top with the ham and pineapple, then the cheese and oregano. Bake for 15–20 minutes until golden brown.

Pumpkin pizza

SERVES 2

4 fl oz (120 ml/½ cup) tomato pasta sauce
2 very small pizza bases
3½ oz (100 g) pumpkin, diced and roasted
1¾ oz (50 g) feta cheese, crumbled
2 sprigs mint, chopped

1. Preheat the oven to 350°F/180°C/Gas mark 4.
2. Spread the tomato sauce over the pizza bases. Top with the roasted pumpkin, feta and mint. Bake for 15–20 minutes until golden brown.

Pumpkin soup with star puffs

SERVES 4

1 tablespoon olive oil
1 small brown (Spanish) onion, chopped
1 leek, chopped
1 clove garlic, crushed
1 lb 12 oz (800 g) butternut pumpkin, peeled
 and cut into ¾ in (2 cm) pieces
1¾ pints (1 litre/4 cups) vegetable stock

1 sheet ready-rolled puff pastry
2 fl oz (50 ml/¼ cup) milk
1 tablespoon sesame seeds
salt and freshly ground black pepper

1. Preheat the oven to 350°F/180°C/Gas mark 4.
2. Heat the oil in a large saucepan over medium heat. Add the onion, leek and garlic. Cook, stirring, for 5 minutes, until the leek is tender.
3. Add the pumpkin and stock. Cover and cook for 20–25 minutes, or until the pumpkin is tender.
4. Meanwhile, using a star-shaped cookie cutter, cut stars from the pastry, brush with milk and scatter with sesame seeds. Place on an baking tray (sheet) and bake for 10–15 minutes until golden and puffed.
5. When the soup is cooked, blend it in batches in a food processor. Return the soup to the saucepan and heat until hot. Season to taste with salt and pepper.

Salami & Swiss melt

MAKES 1

1 piece Turkish bread
1 slice Swiss cheese, cut in half
¾ oz (20 g) baby spinach
4 slices mild salami
1 small tomato, thickly sliced
1 piece roasted bell pepper

1. Preheat a sandwich press.
2. Cut the Turkish bread in half horizontally. Place one half of the Swiss cheese on the one half of the bread, top with spinach, salami, tomato, capsicum and the remaining Swiss cheese. Add the second slice. Cook in the sandwich press until the cheese is melted and the bread toasted.

Cheesy ham pasta bakes

SERVES 4

3½ oz (90 g/1 cup) macaroni
1¾ oz (50 g) sliced ham
2½ oz (70 g) marinated chargrilled bell
  pepper, sliced
1 oz (30 g) mascarpone cheese
salt

4 oz (115 g/½ cup) mozzarella cheese, grated
  (shredded)
¼ bunch chives, chopped

1. Preheat the oven to 400°F/200°C/Gas mark 6.
2. Bring a large saucepan of salted water to the boil, add the macaroni and cook for 8 minutes, or until just firm in the centre (*al dente*). Drain, then return to the pan.
3. Add the ham, bell pepper and mascarpone and gently toss until just combined. Season with salt.
4. Spoon the pasta mixture into four ovenproof dishes and sprinkle with mozzarella. Bake for 10 minutes or until the cheese melts. Remove from the oven and sprinkle with chives.

Homemade baked beans

SERVES 4

1 tablespoon olive oil
1 brown (Spanish) onion, finely chopped
1 clove
14 oz (400 g) can cannellini beans, rinsed
    and drained
14 oz (400 g) can tomatoes, diced
1 tablespoon molasses

1 tablespoon brown sugar
1 bay leaf
salt and freshly ground black pepper
¼ cup parsley, chopped

1. Preheat the oven to 350°F/180°C/Gas mark 4.
2. Heat the oil in a large ovenproof casserole dish over medium heat. Add the onion and cook, stirring, for 3 minutes or until tender. Add the clove, beans, tomatoes, molasses, sugar and bay leaf. Season with salt and pepper. Stir well, then bring to the boil, reduce the heat and simmer for 10 minutes.
3. Cover and bake for 30 minutes or until the sauce is thick. Remove the clove and stir through the parsley.

Frittata

SERVES 4

¹/₃ oz (10 g) butter, plus extra for greasing
½ tablespoon olive oil
½ leek, white part only, thinly sliced
5 oz (150 g) button (white), Swiss brown or
    oyster mushrooms, sliced
3½ oz (100 g) baby spinach
4 eggs

2 fl oz (50 ml) ¼ cup double (heavy) cream
¾ oz (20 g) Parmesan cheese, grated
    (shredded)
1 sprig basil, chopped

1. Preheat the oven to 350°F/180°C/Gas mark 4 and lightly grease a 5½ in (14 cm) square cake tin (pan).
2. Melt the butter with the oil in a large frying pan over medium-low heat. Add the leek and cook for 5 minutes until soft but not browned. Add the mushrooms and spinach and cook for 5 minutes.
3. Meanwhile, whisk together the eggs, cream and Parmesan. Place the leek mixture in the prepared tin, sprinkle with basil and pour over the egg mixture. Bake for 25–30 minutes until lightly browned and set.
4. Cool slightly. Turn onto a board, and cut into squares.

Chicken & risoni soup

SERVES 6

1 small free-range chicken breast
1 tablespoon olive oil
1 small bulb fennel, finely chopped
½ carrot, peeled and finely chopped
½ courgette (zucchini), finely chopped
1 clove garlic, crushed

16 fl oz (475 ml/2 cups) chicken stock
1¼ oz (35 g) risoni (orzo)
1½ oz (40 g) peas
salt and freshly ground black pepper

1. Put the whole chicken in a large pan, cover with water and bring to the boil, turn the heat down and lightly poach for 10 minutes until cooked. Drain and when cool enough to touch, shred.
2. Heat the oil in a large pan over high heat. Add the fennel, carrot, courgette and garlic and cook, stirring, for 5 minutes or until just tender.
3. Add the stock and bring to the boil. Add the risoni and cook, stirring occasionally, for 8 minutes or until pasta is nearly *al dente*.
4. Add the peas and cook for 2 minutes or until bright green and tender. Remove from the heat and stir through the chicken. Season with salt and pepper, to taste.

Lamb koftas

MAKES 10

9 oz (250 g) lean minced (ground) lamb
½ brown (Spanish) onion, finely diced
2 tablespoons couscous
2 sprigs mint, finely chopped
1 sprig parsley, finely chopped

2 teaspoon ground cumin
1 teaspoon ground coriander
1 tablespoon olive oil
pita bread and plain (natural) yogurt, to serve

1. Soak wooden 10 skewers in water for 30 minutes.
2. Combine all the ingredients in a mixing bowl. Mix together well, using your hands.
3. Divide the lamb mixture into heaped tablespoonfuls. Use wet hands to shape each portion into a sausage. Thread each kofta onto a skewer and place on a baking (tray) sheet in a single layer. Cover and refrigerate for 1 hour or until firm.
4. Cook the koftas on a preheated grill (broiler) or chargrill for 8–10 minutes, or until just cooked through. Turn and brush with olive oil occasionally. Serve with pita bread and yogurt.

Eggs in ponchos

SERVES 2

2 rashers (strips) back bacon, diced
3 eggs
2 tablespoons milk
black pepper
1 oz (30 g) butter
1½ oz (45 g/¹/₃ cup) canned chilli (red kidney)
  beans
2 wheat tortillas

GUACAMOLE
1 ripe avocado, chopped
1 small tomato, chopped, plus 1 tomato, cut
  into wedges
2 spring onions (scallions), finely chopped
juice of ½ lime
2 sprigs cilantro (coriander), chopped

1. To make the guacamole, put the avocado, chopped tomato, spring onions, lime juice and cilantro in a bowl. Mash with a fork to combine, then cover and set aside.
2. Fry the bacon in its own fat in a frying pan for 3 minutes or until crisp, then set aside.
3. In a small bowl, mix the eggs and milk together with a fork, then season with pepper.
4. Melt the butter in a samll pan. Add the egg mixture and cook, stirring, for 3 minutes or until the egg is scrambled and well cooked. Gently stir in the bacon pieces.
5. Meanwhile, heat the chilli beans in a saucepan for 4–5 minutes. Place a frying pan over a medium heat, then warm the tortillas, one at a time, for 15 seconds on each side. Transfer to plates, top with the scrambled egg and chilli beans, then wrap each tortilla loosely around its filling. Serve with the guacamole and tomato wedges.

Hide & seek

SERVES 2

2 medium baking potatoes
1 tablespoon vegetable oil
2 rashers (strips) back bacon, diced
2 oz (55 g) mature Cheddar cheese, grated
  (shredded)
1 tablespoon crème fraîche
¼ small bunch fresh chives, chopped
salt and black pepper

COLESLAW
3½ oz (100 g) red cabbage, shredded
2 scallions (spring onions), chopped
1 apple, cored and chopped
1 small carrot, grated (shredded)
2 tablespoons mayonnaise

1. Preheat the oven to 425°F/220°C/Gas mark 7. Rub the potato skins with the oil. Bake for 1 hour, or until soft in the centre.
2. Fry the bacon in a frying pan in its own fat for 3 minutes, or until crisp, then set aside.
3. To make the coleslaw, combine the cabbage, spring onions, apple, carrot and mayonnaise, and refrigerate until needed.
4. When the potatoes are baked, slice the top off each and reserve the top. Scoop out the centres and place in a bowl with the cheese, crème fraîche, chives and bacon pieces. Mix well with a fork and season with salt and black pepper. Pile the mixture back into the empty potato skins and return to the oven for 5 minutes to heat through. Replace the reserved potato tops over the filled potatoes and serve with the coleslaw.

Pick-up sticks

MAKES 6

¼ red bell pepper, cut into small pieces
¼ yellow bell pepper, cut into small pieces
4 button (white) mushrooms, quartered
1 small courgette (zucchini), halved lengthwise
   and thickly sliced
3½ oz (100 g) tofu, cubed

MARINADE
1 tablespoon lemon juice
1 teaspoon clear honey

2 tablespoons light soy sauce
black pepper

DIPPING SAUCE
1 teaspoon olive oil
1 small clove garlic, chopped
3 tablespoons plum sauce
1 teaspoon soft light brown sugar
2½ fl oz (75 ml/^{1}/₃ cup) vegetable stock

1. To make the marinade, mix together the lemon juice, honey, soy sauce and black pepper in a large, non-metallic dish. Add the red and yellow bell peppers, mushrooms, courgette and tofu and stir to coat. Refrigerate for 1 hour to marinate.
2. Meanwhile, soak six wooden skewers in water for 10 minutes to prevent them burning under the grill (broiler).
3. Preheat the grill to medium. Thread the vegetables and tofu onto the skewers. Grill for 6 minutes, turning occasionally, until evenly cooked.
4. To make the dipping sauce, heat the oil in a saucepan. Add the garlic and cook, stirring, for 1 minute or until softened. Stir in the plum sauce, sugar and stock and boil rapidly for 5 minutes or until the sauce has reduced and thickened slightly. Allow to cool for a few minutes, then serve with the kebabs.

Tasty tacos

SERVES 4

1 tablespoon vegetable oil
1 large onion, chopped
2 cloves garlic, crushed
1 lb 2 oz (500 g) lean minced (ground) beef
1 oz (30 g) packet taco seasoning mix
3 tablespoons tomato sauce

8 taco shells
4 large lettuce leaves, cut into strips
2 tomatoes, diced
1½ oz (40 g) mature Cheddar cheese, grated
  (shredded)

1. Preheat the oven to 350°F/180°C/Gas mark 4. Pour the oil into the frying pan. Heat over a medium heat until hot. Add the onion and garlic. Cook, stirring, for 5–6 minutes.
2. Add the beef. Cook, stirring, for 5 minutes.
3. Stir in the taco seasoning mix, 4 fl oz (120 ml/½ cup) water and the tomato sauce. Cook, stirring for 5 minutes.
4. Place the taco shells on a baking tray (sheet). Heat in the oven for 5 minutes.
5. Spoon the beef mixture into the taco shells. Top with lettuce, tomato and cheese.

Crunchy fish sticks

MAKES 24

3 medium potatoes, chopped
15 oz (425 g) canned tuna, drained and flaked
1 egg, lightly beaten
6 oz (150 g/3 cups) breadcrumbs, made from
*   stale bread*
vegetable oil, for shallow-frying

1. Boil or steam the potatoes until tender. Place in a bowl and mash until smooth. Add the tuna and egg and mix well to combine.
2. Arrange the breadcrumbs on a plae.
3. Take 2 tablespoons of mixture, shape into a thick finger and press into the breadcrumbs to coat. Repeat with the remaining mixture.
4. Heat ½ in (1 cm) oil in a frying pan over a medium heat until hot, add the fish sticks and cook for 3–4 minutes on each side, or until cooked through and golden. Drain on absorbent paper, cool slightly and serve.

Little fishes

SERVES 2

3½ oz (100 g/½ cup) long grain rice
1 egg
7 oz (200 g) smoked haddock
6 fl oz (175 ml/¾ cup) milk
¾ oz (25 g) cooked prawns (shrimp), peeled
1 teaspoon lemon juice
pinch of nutmeg
pinch of curry powder

¼ cup parsley, chopped
3 tablespoons double (heavy) cream
black pepper
½ oz (15 g) butter, plus extra for greasing
2 slices bread
½ lemon, cut into quarters

1. Combine the rice with 6 fl oz (175 ml/¾ cup) water in a saucepan. Bring to the boil, reduce the heat to low, cover and cook for 15 minutes. Remove the pan from the heat, allow to stand covered for 10 minutes.
2. Meanwhile, hard boil the egg for 10 minutes. Shell under cold water and finely chop.
3. Put the haddock into a saucepan, cover with the milk and poach for 6–8 minutes, until just firm. Drain well, then flake the flesh, removing any bones and skin.
4. Preheat the oven to 350°F/180°C/Gas mark 4.
5. Place the egg, fish, rice and prawns in a bowl. Stir in the lemon juice, nutmeg, curry powder, parsley, cream and black pepper. Transfer to a greased ovenproof dish. Dot the butter over the top, cover and cook for 25 minutes.
6. Meanwhile, toast the bread, then cut out fish shapes. Serve the rice dish with lemon wedges and the fish-shaped toasts.

Starfish & sea chest

SERVES 2

2 waxy potatoes, cut into ½ in (1 cm)-thick
   chips
3½ oz (100 g) floury potatoes, diced
3½ oz (100 g) skinless cod fillets
4 fl oz (120 ml/½ cup) milk
½ cup parsley, finely chopped
black pepper

1 small egg, beaten
2 tablespoons fresh breadcrumbs
3 tablespoons sunflower oil
4 oz (115 g) green cabbage, finely shredded

1. Place the waxy potatoes in a bowl of water.
2. Boil the floury potato for 10 minutes or until tender, then drain and mash.
3. Place the cod in a saucepan and cover with the milk. Poach for 5 minutes or until firm, then drain and flake, removing any bones.
4. Mix together the mashed potato, cod, parsley and black pepper. Divide the mixture in half and mould each half into a star shape, using your hands or a 3 in (7.5 cm) star-shaped cookie cutter.
5. Place the egg in a shallow dish. Put the breadcrumbs on a plate
6. Dip the starfish into the egg, then the breadcrumbs.
7. Heat 1 tablespoon of the oil in a large, non-stick frying pan and fry the starfish for 5–7 minutes, turning once, until cooked and golden. Drain on absorbent paper and keep warm.
8. Heat the remaining oil in the frying pan until hot but not smoking. Drain the waxy potatoes, then dry the chips in a clean kitchen towel. Fry for 7–10 minutes, until cooked and golden, then drain on absorbent paper.
9. Meanwhile, steam the cabbage for 4–5 minutes until tender. To serve, build a square of chips to make a sea chest, then arrange the cabbage around the starfish like seaweed.

Speedy salmon rissoles

SERVES 4

3 large potatoes, cooked and mashed
14 oz (400 g) can pink salmon, drained and
    flaked
5 oz (150 g) pumpkin, grated (shredded)
3 scallions (spring onions), chopped
1 tablespoon mild mustard
1 tablespoon natural (plain) yogurt

1 egg white
2 teaspoons lemon juice
4 oz (115 g) wholemeal (wholewheat)
    breadcrumbs, made from stale bread
2 teaspoons vegetable oil

1. Put the cooked potatoes, salmon, pumpkin, scallions, mustard, yogurt, egg white and lemon juice in a bowl and mix to combine. Shape the mixture into eight patties and roll in breadcrumbs to coat. Place the patties on a plate, cover and chill for 30 minutes.
2. Heat the oil in a frying pan over medium heat, add the patties and fry for 3–4 minutes each side, or until golden.

Satay vegetables

SERVES 2–4

2 teaspoons vegetable oil
12 snowpeas (mangetout), trimmed and
  halved
15 oz (425 g) can baby sweetcorn
2 oz (55 g) broccoli, chopped
½ oz (15 g) bean sprouts
¼ red bell pepper (capsicum), chopped

2 oz (55 g) peanut butter
1 tablespoon soy sauce
noodles, to serve

1. Heat the oil in a frying pan over a medium heat, add the snowpeas, sweetcorn, broccoli, bean sprouts and red pepper and stir-fry for 3 minutes.
2. Add the peanut butter, soy sauce and 2 fl oz (50 ml/¼ cup) water and cook, stirring, for 4 minutes longer or until vegetables are tender. Serve with noodles.

Tomato shells

MAKES 2

2 tomatoes, halved
2 oz (65 g/¹/₃ cup) rice, cooked
¼ green bell pepper (capsicum), chopped
4 dried apricots, chopped
½ avocado, chopped
1 tablespoon mayonnaise

1. Cut off the tops of the tomatoes and scoop out the flesh, leaving the shells intact. Chop the tops and place in a bowl with the seeds.
2. Add the rice, bell pepper, apricots, avocado and mayonnaise and toss to combine. Spoon the filling into the shells.

Egg foo yung with peas

SERVES 2

2 oz (55 g) snowpeas (mangetout), trimmed
2 oz (55 g) sugar snap peas, trimmed
3 eggs
½ teaspoon soy sauce
1 teaspoon sesame oil
1 tablespoon vegetable oil
1 oz (30 g) bean sprouts
1 scallion (spring onion), finely chopped

1. Boil or steam the snowpeas and sugar snaps until just tender, 2 or 3 minutes. Drain, then refresh under cold running water, drain again and pat dry with absorbent paper.
2. Put the eggs, 2 fl oz (50 ml/¼ cup) water, the soy sauce and sesame oil in a bowl and whisk lightly to combine. Heat the vegetable oil in a frying pan over a medium heat, add the egg mixture and stir-fry for 1 minute, or until the egg just begins to set. Add the snowpeas, sugarsnaps, bean sprouts and scallion and stir-fry for 1 minute longer. Cool slightly and serve.

Vegetable risotto

SERVES 4

8 fl oz (250 ml/1 cup) tomato or vegetable
    juice
4 fl oz (120 ml/½ cup) vegetable or chicken
    stock
1 tablespoon vegetable oil
1 small onion, chopped
4 oz (115 g) carrots, finely diced or grated
    (shredded)

2 oz (55 g) button (white) mushrooms, sliced
1 cup arborio rice
3 oz (85 g) courgette (zucchini), sliced
¼ red or green bell pepper (capsicum), sliced
1½ oz (45g) mature Cheddar cheese, grated
    (shredded)
pine nuts or sesame seeds, toasted

1. Combine the juice and stock in a saucepan and bring to a simmer over medium heat
2. Heat the oil in a saucepan over a medium heat, add the onion, carrots and mushrooms and cook, stirring, for 3–4 minutes or until the onion is soft. Add the rice, courgette and bell pepper to the saucepan and cook over a medium heat, stirring constantly, for 3 minutes, or until rice becomes translucent.
3. Pour 4 fl oz (120 ml/½ cup) hot stock into the rice mixture and cook, stirring constantly, until the liquid is absorbed. Continue cooking in this way until all the stock is used and the rice is tender. Scatter cheese and pine nuts or sesame seeds on top and serve.

Creamy vegetable pasta

SERVES 2

4 oz (115 g) pasta bows
2 teaspoons vegetable oil
4 oz (115 g) cauliflower, chopped
4 oz (115 g) broccoli, chopped
1 courgette (zucchini), chopped
1 carrot, chopped or grated (shredded)
4 oz (115g) cream cheese, softened
3 tablespoons milk

1. Bring a large pan of salted water to the boil, add the pasta and cook for 8 minutes, or until just firm in the centre (*al dente*). Drain, set aside and keep warm.
2. Meanwhile heat the oil in a frying pan over medium heat, add the cauliflower, broccoli, courgette and carrot and cook, stirring, for 3–4 minutes, or until vegetables are just tender.
3. Stir the cream cheese and milk into the pan and, stirring, bring to simmering. Simmer for 4 minutes. Spoon the vegetable mixture over the pasta and serve.

Mushroom penne

SERVES 1

4 oz (115 g) penne
1 tablespoon olive oil
4 oz (115 g) button (white) mushrooms, sliced
2 tablespoons vegetable stock
2 tablespoons sour cream
8 sprigs fresh parsley, chopped

1. Bring a large pan of salted water to the boil, add the penne and cook for 8 minutes, or until just firm in the centre (*al dente*). Drain, set aside and keep warm.
2. Meanwhile, heat the oil in a frying pan over medium heat, add the mushrooms and cook, stirring, for 4 minutes. Add the stock and sour cream to the pan and cook for 2 minutes longer. Stir in the parsley and spoon thee sauce over the pasta. Toss to combine and serve.

special food

Brown rice salad

SERVES 4

5 oz (150 g/¾ cup) brown rice
1 tablespoon pine nuts, toasted
3½ oz (100 g/⅓ cup) sunflower seeds
1 teaspoon ground cumin
2 tablespoons currants
1 scallion (spring onion), sliced
2 sprigs cilantro (coriander), chopped

DRESSING
zest of ½ orange
1 tablespoon fresh orange juice
1 tablespoon olive oil

1. Bring a large pan of water to the boil, add the brown rice and cook for 25–30 minutes until tender. Drain, rinse under cold running water, drain again and place in a large bowl.
2. Add the pine nuts, sunflower seeds, cumin, currants, scallion and cilantro.
3. To make the dressing, place all the ingredients in a small bowl, whisk to combine and pour over the salad.

Pumpkin & fig salad

SERVE 4

9 oz (250 g) butternut pumpkin, cut into ¾ in
  (2 cm) pieces
1 teaspoon ground cumin
2 tablespoons olive oil
salt
7 oz (200 g) can chickpeas, drained and rinsed
4 dried figs, chopped
½ small red onion, thinly sliced
1¾ oz (50 g) baby spinach
2 sprigs parsley, chopped
1 tablespoon lemon juice

1. Preheat the oven to 400°F/200°C/Gas mark 6. Combine the pumpkin, cumin and 1 tablespoon of the oil in a bowl. Season with salt and place in a roasting dish. Roast for 10 minutes or until tender, then allow to cool.
2. Combine the pumpkin, chickpeas, figs, onion, spinach and parsley in a large bowl. Toss until well combined. Pour over the lemon juice and remaining oil before packing into a lunchbox.

Quinoa salad

SERVES 4

1½ oz (45 g/¼ cup) quinoa
1 oz (30 g) green beans, cut into ¾ in (2 cm)
  pieces
1 tomato, diced
¼ cup mint, finely chopped
1 tablespoon olive oil
1 teaspoon lemon juice

1. Rinse the quinoa in cold water. Drain and place in a pan with 4 fl oz (120 ml/½ cup) water, bring to the boil and simmer for 10 minutes until tender. Drain and leave to cool.
2. Bring a small pan of water to the boil and blanch the beans, drain and refresh.
3. Mix the tomato, mint and beans through the quinoa. Stir through the oil and lemon juice.

Buckwheat noodle salad

SERVES 2

1¾ oz (50 g) buckwheat noodles
1 oz (30 g) snowpeas (mangetout), cut into
  batons
1 small carrot, cut into batons
¼ red bell pepper (capsicum), cut into
  thin slices

¼ green bell pepper (capsicum), cut into
  thin slices
1 teaspoon sesame oil
½ teaspoon sesame seeds
2 sprigs cilantro (coriander), chopped

1. Bring a pan of water to the boil, add the buckwheat noodles and cook for
   5 minutes, or until just firm in the centre (*al dente*). Rinse under cold water
   and drain, then transfer to a bowl.
2. Add the remaining ingredients and mix well.

Corn bread

MAKES 1 LOAF

½ teaspoon olive oil
1 red bell pepper (capsicum), finely chopped
1 teaspoon ground cumin
5 oz (150 g/1¼ cups) self-rising (self-raising) flour
3 oz (85 g/¾ cup) cornmeal (polenta)
1 teaspoon baking powder

½ teaspoon salt
4 oz (115 g) corn kernels
¼ cup cilantro (coriander), finely chopped
8 fl oz (250 ml/1 cup) milk
1½ oz (40 g) butter, melted and cooled
1 egg, lightly whisked

1. Preheat the oven to 425°F/220°C/Gas mark 7. Lightly spray an 8 x 21 cm (3¼ x 8¼ in) loaf tin (pan) with olive oil spray.
2. Heat the oil in a non-stick frying pan over medium-high heat. Add the capsicum and cook, stirring, for 5 minutes or until tender. Add the cumin and cook, stirring, for 1 minute or until aromatic. Set aside for 5 minutes to cool slightly.
3. Combine the flour, cornmeal, baking powder and salt in a large bowl. Add the corn, cilantro and bell pepper mixture, and stir until well combined. Add the milk, melted butter and egg, and use a wooden spoon to mix until well combined.
4. Pour into the loaf tin and smooth the surface with the back of a spoon. Bake for 30–35 minutes or until a skewer inserted into the centre of the loaf comes out clean. Leave to set for 5 minutes before turning onto a wire rack to go cold.

Bean & bacon salad

SERVES 4

1 oz (30 g) green beans, cut in to ¾ in (2 cm)
   pieces
3 rashers (strips) bacon, sliced
7 oz (200 g) can cannellini beans
7 oz (200 g) can borlotti beans
½ red onion, finely chopped
8 cherry tomatoes, quartered
¼ cup parsley, chopped
¼ cup mint, chopped

DRESSING
1 teaspoon wholegrain mustard
2 tablespoons orange juice
2 tablespoons olive oil

1. Bring a large pan of water to the boil, blanch the beans, refresh in cold water and place in a bowl.
2. Fry the bacon in its own fat in a non-stick frying pan until golden brown, then drain on absorbent paper. Add to the beans.
3. Rinse and drain the cannellini and borlotti beans, add to the bacon and green beans. Add the onion, tomato, parsley and mint. Mix to combine.
4. To make the dressing, whisk the ingredients together in a bowl. Drizzle over the dish.

Chicken & cabbage salad

SERVES 4

1 cooked chicken breast, shredded
$^1/_8$ red cabbage, finely shredded
¼ baby wombok (Chinese cabbage), finely shredded
1 carrot, grated (shredded)
2 sprigs parsley, chopped
1 orange
½ teaspoon Dijon mustard
2 tablespoons oil

1. Combine the chicken, red cabbage, wombok, carrot and parsley in a bowl and mix well.
2. With a sharp knife, peel the orange to remove all the skin and pith, and trim away the outer skin on the segments. Working over a bowl to save the juices, remove the segments by cutting along each side of each segment, between the skin and the flesh. Add the segments to the chicken and cabbage.
3. Combine the orange juice, mustard and oil in a bowl, stir together and pour over the salad.

Rice paper rolls

MAKES 16

1 ¾ oz (50 g) vermicelli rice noodles
1 carrot, cut into thin strips
1 cucumber, deseeded and cut into thin strips
½ cup cilantro (coriander)
1 tablespoon sweet chilli sauce

3½ oz (100 g) firm tofu, cut into strips
16 small rice paper sheets

1. Soak the noodles in boiling water for 5 minutes until soft, then drain and place in a bowl.
2. Add the carrot, cucumber, cilantro and sweet chilli sauce and mix together until combined.
3. Pour hot water into a shallow bowl, place the rice paper in the water for about 30 seconds until soft. Gently lift out and place on a clean, flat surface.
4. In the centre of 1 wrapper, place some noodle mix and top with some of the tofu strips. Roll the rice paper, sealing with a little water. Place on a tray and cover with a clean, damp kitchen towel to keep moist. Repeat with the remaining rice paper sheets.

Beetroot dip

SERVES 4

1 medium beetroot, root and stem trimmed
1 cup natural (plain) yogurt
2 cloves garlic, crushed
1 sprig fresh thyme, leaves removed and stalk
  discarded

pinch of salt
vegetable sticks, to serve

1. Place the unpeeled beetroot in a medium pan and cover with plenty of cold water. Bring to the boil, reduce the heat to medium and cook for 20 minutes or until tender. Drain and set aside until cool enough to handle.
2. Wear kitchen gloves to avoid staining your hands, and peel the beetroot. Set aside until cooled to room temperature.
3. Cut the beetroot into large pieces, place in a food processor and process until smooth. Add the yogurt, garlic and thyme, and process until well combined. Season with salt. Serve with carrot and celery sticks. Keep any leftover dip in the refrigerator.

sweet treats

Apple crumble

SERVES 6

3 cooking apples

CRUMBLE TOPPING
6 oz (175 g/¾ cup) brown sugar
2 oz (55 g/½ cup) plain (all-purpose) flour
2½ oz (75 g/¾ cup) rolled oats
2 oz (55 g) butter, plus extra for greasing

1. Preheat the oven to 350°F/180°C/Gas mark 4.
2. Peel the apples, cut into quarters and remove the cores. Slice thinly. Place the apple slices in lightly greased ovenproof dish.
3. To make the topping, put the sugar, flour and rolled oats in a large bowl. Chop the butter into pieces. Add to the bowl. Using your fingers, mix in the butter until the mixture is the consistency of breadcrumbs. Sprinkle the topping over the apples.
4. Bake for 35 minutes until golden.

Apple roll-ups

SERVES 2

2 oz (55 g) plain (all-purpose) flour
¼ pint (150 ml) milk
1 egg
zest of 1 orange, finely grated (shredded)
1 oz (30 g) butter, melted, plus extra for frying
maple syrup and vanilla ice cream, to serve

FOR THE FILLING
2 eating apples, peeled, cored and diced
½ teaspoon ground cinnamon (powder)
1 tablespoon water

1. To make the batter, blend the flour, milk, egg, orange zest and melted butter until smooth in a food processor, or using a hand blender. Set aside to rest for 20 minutes.
2. Meanwhile, make the filling. Put the apples, cinnamon and 1 tablespoon of water into a small saucepan, cover, and cook gently for 5–7 minutes, stirring occasionally, until the apples have softened.
3. Melt just enough butter to cover the base of an 7 in (18 cm) non-stick frying pan. Pour in a quarter of the batter and tilt the pan so that it covers the base. Cook for 1–2 minutes on each side, until golden. Keep warm and repeat to make 3 more pancakes, greasing the pan when necessary.
4. Place 2 pancakes on each plate. Fill with the apple mixture and carefully roll up. Serve with maple syrup. Try them with a scoop of vanilla ice cream.

Fruit & jelly wedges

SERVES 6–8

14 oz (400 g) can fruit of your choice in
 unsweetened juice
2 tablespoons gelatine dissolved in 4 fl oz
 (120 ml/½ cup) hot water, cooled

food colouring of your choice (optional)
3–4 oranges

1. Drain the canned fruit and reserve the juice.
2. Combine the gelatine mixture and the reserved juice in a measuring jug (pitcher) and make up to 16 fl oz (475 ml/2 cups) with water. Add a few drops of food colouring, if desired. Stir well to combine, then refrigerate until the mixture just begins to thicken.
3. Cut the oranges in half and scoop out the pulp with a spoon, leaving the orange shells intact.
4. Fold the drained fruit into the jelly and spoon the mixture into the orange shells. Place the shells on a tray and refrigerate for 2–3 hours, or until the jelly is set. To serve, cut each jelly-filled orange shell into three wedges.

Syrup bananas

SERVES 4

2 oz (55 g) unsalted butter
2½ oz (65 g/¹/₃ cup) brown sugar
½ teaspoon ground cinnamon
4 bananas, halved lengthwise
2 fl oz (50 ml/¼ cup) banana-flavoured syrup
4 fl oz (120 ml/½ cup) orange juice
4 scoops vanilla ice cream

1. Melt the butter in a heavy pan over a medium heat. Add the sugar and cinnamon and cook, stirring, until the sugar melts and the mixture is combined.
2. Stir in the orange juice and the banana-flavoured syrup. Cook for 5 minutes or until the mixture is thick and syrupy.
3. Add the bananas and toss to coat with syrup. To serve, divide the bananas and ice cream between the serving plates and drizzle the sauce from the pan over the ice cream. Serve immediately.

Grape slushie swirl

SERVES 2

2 ice blocks
4 oz (115 g/1 cup) seedless green grapes,
   frozen
¼ teaspoon fresh ginger pulp
1 teaspoon white (granulated) sugar
4 oz (115 g/1 cup) seedless red grapes, frozen
2 tablespoons fig jam

1. Blend 1 ice block, the green grapes, ginger pulp and sugar in a blender until slushy and all combined. Decant into a chilled bowl and place in the freezer.
2. Blend the other ice block, red grapes and fig jam until slushy and all combined. Decant into a chilled bowl.
3. Spoon each coloured mixture into serving glasses, a few scoops of each colour at a time until glasses are full.

Apricot & coconut balls

MAKES 12

4 oz (115 g/½ cup) honey
8 oz (225 g/1 cup) dried apricots, chopped
1½ oz (40 g/¼ cup) dates, chopped
4½ oz (130 g/1½ cups) desiccated (dry
* unsweetened shredded) coconut*

1. Place the honey, apricots, dates and two-thirds of the coconut in a food processor and blend together.
2. Roll heaped tablespoonfuls of mixture into balls and roll in the remaining coconut. Store in the refrigerator.

Fruit bubble bumps

MAKES 12

7 oz (200 g) butter
4 tablespoons honey
4 ½ oz (135 g/4½ cups) rice bubbles or
*   rice krispies*
3 oz (85 g/½ cup) dates, chopped
¼ cup dried apple, chopped

1. Line a 12-cup muffin tray with paper cases.
2. Put the butter and honey in a small saucepan, bring to the boil and simmer for 5 minutes.
3. Combine the rice bubbles and chopped fruit in a large bowl. Pour over the butter mixture and stir to combine.
4. Divide the mixture between the cupcake cases. Refrigerate until firm. Store in an airtight container.

Strawberry & ricotta muffins

SERVES 12

10 oz (300 g/2½ cups) self-rising (self-raising) flour
1 teaspoon ground cinnamon
4½ oz (135 g/²/₃ cup superfine (caster) sugar
2 eggs

2 oz (55 g) unsalted butter, melted
8 fl oz (250 ml/1 cup) milk
9 oz (250 g) ricotta cheese
9 oz (250 g) strawberries, quartered

1. Preheat the oven to 350°F/180°C/Gas mark 4 and line a 12-cup muffin tray with paper cases.
2. Sift the flour and cinnamon into a large bowl. Add the sugar and stir to combine.
3. Place the eggs, butter and milk in another bowl and whisk to combine. Add to the dry ingredients and stir until just combined. Stir the ricotta and strawberries into the mixture, then divide between the paper cases.
4. Bake for 20–25 minutes, or until golden.

Muddy puddles

MAKES 4

2½ oz (75 g) chocolate digestive biscuits
   (cookies)
2½ oz (75 g) butter
2½ oz (75 g) milk chocolate
2 tablespoons golden (corn) syrup
1 egg, beaten

few drops of vanilla extract
½ oz (15 g) white chocolate

1. Put the biscuits into a plastic bag, seal, then crush with a rolling pin.
2. Melt 1 oz (30 g) of the butter in a small pan. Remove from the heat and mix in the biscuits.
3. Line a muffin tray with 4 paper muffin cases. Divide the biscuit mixture between them, pressing over the base and sides of each case with the back of a teaspoon. Refrigerate for 20 minutes or until firm.
4. Preheat the oven to 350°F/180°C/Gas mark 4.
5. Put the remaining butter, milk chocolate and golden syrup in a bowl set over a pan of simmering water. Heat gently, stirring, until melted. Remove from the heat and leave to cool for 5 minutes. Whisk in the egg and vanilla.
6. Spoon the chocolate mixture over the bases and bake for 20 minutes, or until just firm. Leave to cool for 10 minutes.
7. Meanwhile, melt the white chocolate in a bowl set over a pan of simmering water, then drizzle over the puddles.

Chocolate brownies

MAKES 12

7 oz (200 g) unsalted butter, chopped
7 oz (200 g) dark (bittersweet) chocolate,
    broken into pieces
8 oz (225 g/1 cup) brown sugar
3 oz (85 g/¾ cup) plain (all-purpose) flour
2 tablespoons unsweetened cocoa powder

3 oz (85 g/¾ cup) walnuts, chopped
3 eggs, lightly beaten
1 teaspoon vanilla extract
2 oz (55 g/¼ cup) confectioners' (icing) sugar

1. Preheat the oven to 375°F/190°C/Gas mark 5. Grease and line a deep, 7 in (18 cm) square cake tin (pan) with baking paper.
2. Heat the butter, chocolate and sugar in a saucepan over low heat, stirring constantly, until melted and smooth. Transfer to a bowl and set aside to cool slightly.
3. Sift the flour and cocoa into a bowl, stir through the walnuts. Add the eggs and vanilla and mix well. Fold the dry ingredients through the chocolate mixture.
4. Pour the brownie batter into the cake tin. Bake for 40–45 minutes or until just set, then leave to cool. Once cooled, lift out of tin and wrap in cling wrap (cling film). Place in an airtight container. Stand for 1 day before dusting with the icing sugar and cutting into pieces.

Banana muffins

MAKES 12

7 oz (200 g/1¾ cups) wholemeal
* (wholewheat) self-rising (self-raising) flour*
6 oz (150 g/¾ cup) firmly packed brown sugar
1 oz (30 g/¼ cup) walnut pieces
2 bananas, mashed
1 egg, lightly beaten
8 fl oz (250 ml/1 cup) buttermilk
²/₃ oz (20 g) butter, melted, plus extra for
* greasing*

1. Preheat the oven to 350°F/180°C/Gas mark 4 and grease a 12-cup muffin tray.
2. Sift the flour and sugar into a bowl, stir through the walnut pieces. Mix the banana, egg, buttermilk and butter in a separate bowl. Add to the dry ingredients and stir to just combine.
3. Divide the mixture between the muffin cups and bake for 20–25 minutes. Test to make sure the muffins are cooked by inserting a skewer into the centre of one. If it comes out clean the muffins are baked. Leave to set for 5 minutes, then turn onto a wire rack to go cold.

Butter cookies

MAKES 48

4 oz (115 g) butter, plus extra for greasing
4 oz (115 g) ghee
9 oz (250 g/1¼ cups) caster (superfine) sugar
½ teaspoon ground cinnamon (powder)
3 eggs
1½ teaspoons baking powder

1 lb (450 g/4 cups) plain (all-purpose) flour
sesame seeds
1 egg mixed with a little milk to make an egg
   glaze

1. Preheat the oven to 380°F/190°C/Gas mark 5.
2. In a large bowl, cream the butter, ghee and sugar until well combined, then stir in the cinnamon and the eggs, beating mixture well.
3. Add the baking powder, then begin to add the flour. Mix in a little at a time until the desired consistency is reached. Test to see if dough is right by rolling a little in your hands – if it is not sticky, and rolls well, enough flour has been added.
4. Shape the pieces of dough into slim pencil-shapes, roll in the sesame seeds, then form into scrolls. Place on greased baking sheet, brush with egg glaze and bake for 15–20 minutes. Leave to set for a few minutes then turn out on to a wire rack to go cold.

Fruit salad

SERVES 2

4 oz (115g) strawberries, halved
¼ pineapple, cut into chunks
1 banana, cut into chunks
½ mango, cut into chunks
4 oz (115g) blueberries

2 passionfruit
juice of 1 orange
1 sprig mint, chopped

1. Place the strawberries, pineapple, banana, mango and blueberries in a bowl.
2. Cut the passionfruit in half, scoop out the pulp and add to the fruit. Pour over the orange juice and mix in the mint leaves.

Marzipan triangles

MAKES 42

3½ oz (90 g/1 cup) rolled oats
4 oz (115 g/½ cup) caster (superfine) sugar
4 oz (115 g/1 cup) self-rising (self-raising) flour, sifted
3 oz (85 g/¾ cup) ground almonds (almond meal)
1 tablespoon golden (corn) syrup
4 fl oz (120 ml/½ cup) canola oil
1 egg
¼ teaspoon almond extract
⅓ cup flaked almonds, to decorate

MARZIPAN
4 oz (115 g/1 cup) ground almonds (almond meal)
1½ oz (40 g/⅓ cup) icing (confectioners') sugar
1¾ oz (50 g/¼ cup caster (superfine) sugar
3 teaspoons egg white (about ½ an egg white)
¼ teaspoon almond extract or ½ teaspoon amaretto liqueur
few drops orange blossom water or pure vanilla extract

1. To make the marzipan, sift the almonds and sugars into a bowl. Add the egg white, almond extract and orange water. Mix to a smooth stiff paste. Wrap in cling wrap (cling film). Chill until required.
2. Combine the oats, sugar, flour and ground almonds in a bowl.
3. Combine the golden syrup, oil, egg and almond extract in another bowl. Stir into the oats mixture. Spread half the mixture evenly over the base of a greased and lined 8 x 12 in (20 x 30 cm) cake tin (pan).
4. Preheat the oven to 360°F/180°C/Gas mark 4. Roll out the marzipan and to fit the cake tin and press over the cake batter. Top with remaining oats mixture. Sprinkle with chopped almonds. Press into mixture.
5. Bake for 30 minutes or until golden. Leave to set for 10 minutes, then turn out onto a wire rack to go cold. Cut into triangles, to serve.

Walnut chocolate slice

MAKES 25

4 egg whites
2 oz (55 g/¼ cup) sugar
4 oz (115 g) chocolate, melted and cooled
3 oz (85 g) butter, melted and cooled, plus
    extra for greasing
1½ teaspoons vanilla extract
4 oz (115 g/1 cup) plain (all-purpose) flour
2 oz (55 g/¼ cup) brown sugar

4½ oz (135 g/⅓ cup) unsweetened cocoa
    powder
2 teaspoons baking powder
½ teaspoon baking soda (bicarbonate of soda)
1½ oz (40 g/⅓ cup) chopped walnuts or
    pecans
fresh berries, to serve (optional)

1. Preheat the oven to 380°C/190°C/Gas mark 5. Grease and line a 9 in (23 cm) square cake tin (pan).
2. Beat the egg whites in a large grease-free bowl until soft peaks form. Gradually beat in the sugar until it dissolves. Fold in the melted chocolate, cooled butter and vanilla extract.
3. Sift the flour, brown sugar, cocoa, baking powder and baking soda into another large bowl. Make a well in the centre. Fold in the egg whites and walnuts until just combined. Spoon into the prepared tin.
4. Bake for 20–25 minutes, or until a skewer inserted into the centre comes out clean. Leave to cool in the tin.
5. Cut into 1½–2 in (4–5 cm) bars. Serve with fresh berries, if desired.

Raspberry yogurt slice

MAKES 15

3½ oz (100 g) butter
4 oz (115 g/1 cup) plain (all-purpose) flour
2 oz (55 g/¼ cup) brown sugar
2¼ oz (65 g/¾ cup) rolled oats

TOPPING
4 oz (125 g) cream cheese
6 oz (175 g/¾ cup) raspberry yogurt

1 tablespoon honey
1 teaspoon lemon juice
1 teaspoon lemon zest, grated (shredded)
1 tablespoon gelatine
8 oz (225 g) frozen raspberries
2 oz (55 g/¼ cup) sugar
fresh raspberries, to serve

1. Preheat the oven to 360°F/180°C/Gas mark 4. Grease and line a 11 x 7 in (28 x 18 cm) cake tin (pan).
2. Blend the butter and flour with the sugar in a food processor until the dough just comes together. Fold in the oats.
3. Press into the base of the prepared tin and bake for about 15–20 minutes or until a skewer comes out clean when inserted into the cake centre. Leave to set for a few minutes before turning out on to a wire rack to go cold.
4. In a bowl, beat the cream cheese with the yogurt and honey. Add the lemon juice and zest. Set aside in the refrigerator
5. In a small bowl pour the gelatine over 2 fl ox (50 ml/¼ cup) water to soften.
6. Heat three-quarters of the thawed raspberries in a saucepan and add the sugar and softened gelatine. Bring to the boil, stirring until the sugar and gelatine have thoroughly dissolved. Press through a sieve into a clean bowl, and leave to cool until thickened slightly. Stir into the creamed cheese and yogurt mixture with the remaining raspberries.
7. Pour the yogurt mixture over the sponge base and refrigerate overnight. Serve with extra raspberries.

Flourless orange cake

SERVES 8

oil, for greasing
2 oranges
3 eggs
7 oz (225 g/1 cup) caster (superfine) sugar
12 oz (250 g/3 cups) ground almonds (almond meal)
1 teaspoon baking powder

1. Preheat the oven to 350°F/180°C/Gas mark 4. Lightly grease and line a 22 cm (8 ½in) round springform tin (pan).
2. Place the whole oranges in a large pan and cover with cold water. Bring to the boil over medium heat. Cook for 15 minutes or until tender. Drain, then return to the pan and cover with cold water. Bring to the boil and cook for 15 minutes. Drain. Chop the oranges, discarding any seeds. Place the oranges in a food processor and process until smooth.
3. Use an electric beater to whisk the eggs and sugar together in a large bowl until thick and pale. Add the oranges, almond meal and baking powder and gently fold until just combined. Pour into the prepared tin.
4. Bake for 1 hour. Test with a skewer to make sure cake is baked. If the skewer comes out clean the cake is ready. Leave to set for 15 minutes then turn out on to a wire rack to go cold.

Pancake stacks

MAKES 10

*2½ oz (75 g/²⁄₃ cup) self-raising (self-rising)
  flour*
2 tablespoons sugar
1 egg
¼ pint (150 ml/²⁄₃ cup) milk

1 oz (30 g) butter
maple syrup, to serve

1. Sift the flour into a large mixing bowl. Add the sugar.
2. In another bowl, whis the egg and milk together.
3. Make a well in the centre of the flour mixture. Pour in the egg mixture. Beat with wooden spoon until smooth.
4. Place a little butter in frying pan. Heat over a medium-high heat until melted and sizzling.
5. Pour 3–4 tablespoons of batter into the frying pan. Swirl around the pan quickly to coat it. Cook until bubbles form on top of the pancake. Turn over. Cook for 1–2 minutes or until the second side is brown.
6. Place the cooked pancakes on a plate. Repeat with remaining pancake batter.
7. Stack three or four pancakes on each serving plate. Serve with a drizzle of maple syrup.

Honey macadamia shortbread

MAKES 24

2 oz (55 g/½ cup) macadamias
4 oz (115 g/1 cup) plain (all-purpose) flour
2 oz (55 g/½ cup) cornflour (cornstarch)
¼ teaspoon salt
1½ oz (40 g/¼ cup) caster (superfine) sugar
4 oz (115 g) butter
2 tablespoons honey

1. Finely chop half the macadamias. Cut the remainder in half and set aside.
2. Sift the flours, salt and sugar together into a large bowl. Rub in the butter until the mixture is like breadcrumbs, then stir in the honey and chopped macadamia nuts.
3. Turn onto a lightly floured board and knead lightly. Roll out to ½ in (12 mm) thickness and place in the refrigerator for about 10 minutes. Preheat the oven to 400°F/200C/Gas mark 6.
4. before cutting into rounds using a 2 in (5 cm) fluted cookie cutter. Place half a nut on each round.
5. Place the shortbreads on a greased baking tray (sheet) and bake for about 15 minutes, or until golden brown.

Baked fresh dates & apples

SERVES 4

5 large cooking apples
7 oz (200 g) fresh dates, pitted and halved
juice of ½ lemon
juice of 2 oranges
zest of 1 orange, finely grated (shredded)
2 cinnamon sticks
3 tablespoons clear honey
Greek yogurt, to serve

1. Preheat the oven to 360°F/180°C/Gas mark 4. Lightly grease an ovenproof dish.
2. Peel and thinly slice the apples and arrange in the prepared dish. Stir in the dates, juices, zest and cinnamon sticks. Drizzle the honey over the mixture.
3. Cover and bake for 45–55 minutes (until tender and the flavours are absorbed).
4. Serve warm or chilled with Greek yogurt, dusted with cinnamon.

smoothies

Banana smoothie

SERVES 2

4 fl oz (120 ml/½ cup) milk
2–3 drops vanilla extract
1½ bananas
grating of nutmeg (optional)
4 fl oz (120 ml/½ cup) plain (natural) yogurt
4 ice cubes
1 teaspoon honey

1. Place all the ingredients except for the nutmeg in a blender; blend until smooth. Pour into chilled glasses and serve topped with a grating of nutmeg.

Banana and berry smoothie

SERVES 2

4 fl oz (120 ml/½ cup) milk
5–6 blueberries
½ banana
4 fl oz (120 ml/½ cup) plain (natural) yogurt
2 strawberries
1 teaspoon honey
½ apple, peeled
3 ice cubes

1. Place all the ingredients in a blender; blend until smooth. Pour into chilled glasses and serve topped with coloured sprinkles.

Berry smoothie

SERVES 2

4 fl oz (120 ml/½ cup) milk
1 teaspoon honey
1 banana
2 drops of vanilla extract
6 frozen strawberries
vanilla sugar (made by infusing a vanilla pod
   (bean) in caster (superfine) sugar

10–12 blueberries
4 ice cubes

1. Place all the ingredients except for the sugar in a blender; blend until smooth. Pour into chilled glasses and serve topped with a fresh strawberry, a few blueberries and a sprinkle of vanilla sugar.

Hawaiian delight smoothie

SERVES 2

4 fl oz (120 ml/½ cup) milk
1 teaspoon honey
6 cherries
2–3 drops vanilla extract
5 oz (150 g) pineapple cubes
pink sprinkles
½ mandarin
2 ice cubes
4 fl oz (120 ml/½ cup) plain (natural) yogurt

1. Place all theingredients except for the sprinkles in a blender; blend until smooth. Pour into chilled glasses and serve topped with coloured sprinkles.

Kiwi fruit smoothie

SERVES 2

4 fl oz (120 ml/½ cup) milk
2 teaspoons honey
½ banana, plus extra to decorate
4 ice cubes
2 frozen strawberries
1½ peeled kiwi fruit, plus extra to decorate
½ teaspoon vanilla sugar
4 fl oz (120 ml/½ cup) plain (natural) yogurt

1. Place all the ingredients except for the decoration in a blender; blend until smooth. Pour into chilled glasses and serve topped with a slice of fresh kiwi fruit and banana.

Passion fruit smoothie

SERVES 2

4 fl oz (120 ml/½ cup) milk
pulp of 1 passionfruit, plus extra, to decorate
½ apple
4 fl oz (120 ml/½ cup) plain (natural) yogurt
½ banana
juice of 1 orange
1 teaspoon honey

1. Place all ingredients except for the decoration in a blender; blend until smooth. Pour into chilled glasses and serve topped with a swirl of passionfruit pulp.

Orange & banana smoothie

SERVES 2

4 fl oz (120 ml/½ cup) milk
4 fl oz (120 ml/½ cup) plain (natural) yogurt
1 orange, peeled and deseeded
1 teaspoon honey
½ banana
2–3 drops vanilla extract
2 strawberries
2 ice cubes

1. Place all the ingredients in blender; blend until smooth. Pour into chilled glasses and serve.

Strawberry smoothie

SERVES 2

4 fl oz (120 ml/½ cup) milk
2–3 drops vanilla extract
6 frozen strawberries
pinch of nutmeg (optional)
4 fl oz (120 ml/½ cup) plain (natural) yogurt
1 teaspoon honey
4 blocks of ice
fresh strawberry, to decorate

1. Place all the ingredients except for the fresh strawberry in a blender; blend until smooth. Pour into chilled glasses and serve topped with half a fresh strawberry.

Tropical fruit smoothie

SERVES 2

4 fl oz (120 ml/½ cup) milk
1 teaspoon honey
½ banana
5 oz (125 g) fresh pineapple cubes
2 ice cubes
4 fl oz (120 ml/½ cup) plain (natural) yogurt
2 strawberries, plus extra to decorate
4 fl oz (120 ml/½ cup) coconut milk

1. Place all the ingredients except for the decoration and coconut milk in a blender; blend until smooth. Pour in 4 fl oz (120 ml/½ cup) of coconut milk and stir. Pour into chilled glasses and serve topped with strawberries.

Tropical burst smoothie

SERVES 2

2 fl oz (50 ml/¼ cup) milk
1 kiwi fruit, peeled and quartered
3 strawberries
2½ oz (75 g) watermelon, deseeded
4 fl oz (120 ml/½ cup) plain (natural) yogurt
1 teaspoon honey
2 ice cubes

1. Place all the ingredients in blender; blend until smooth. Pour into chilled
   glasses and serve.

Index

Published in 2014 by
New Holland Publishers
London • Sydney • Cape Town • Auckland

The Chandlery Unit 114 50 Westminster Bridge Road London SE1 7QY
1/66 Gibbes Street Chatswood NSW 2067 Australia
Wembley Square First Floor Solan Road Gardens Cape Town 8001 South Africa
218 Lake Road Northcote Auckland New Zealand

Copyright © 2014 New Holland Publishers

www.newhollandpublishers.com

A catalogue record of this book is available at the British Library and the National
Library of Australia.

ISBN: 9781742574844

Publisher: Fiona Schultz
Design: Lorena Susak
Production Director: Olga Dementiev
Printer: Toppan Leefung Printing Ltd (China)

10 9 8 7 6 5 4 3 2 1

Texture: Shutterstock

Follow New Holland Publishers on
Facebook: www.facebook.com/NewHollandPublishers